Jet Fuel Dreams

Poems by Jessica Mannes

Shoe Music Press

Flight

Jet fuel dreams

High on Altitude and sheer possibility

To have awakened upon the new dawn of a once dead subsistence

Alive in luminous glory

Much to my surprise

Hope and excitement in full bloom

Battle

You've stood to learn just how hard you were born to fight

Just how much you were destined to win

And lose

Do you know, though, the extent of the damage done, direct and collateral, by the energy expended in battle, the blows suffered in return, in your great effort to become reformed?

Pieces from your wit, your will, your worth

Face now the finality that your only opponent, the only one left standing, at the very least, is yourself

And are you a foe to be considered formidable?

One might think so, indeed

For you've swept your battleground clean of adversaries so that you might stand beyond reproach in desolation

Still vigilant, though, in a state of distrust of peace or solitude

Eyes in constant scan of the horizon, to lie in wait and worry

With hopes great, fears greater still, and dreams insurmountable

Resurrection

Where hope has been bred upon a new horizon

Still unfolding in spring's bloom

You found within me the wellspring of words

Avenged my spirit to set them free

Pressed my pen then to pages that filled themselves rapidly with fervor in the act of sweet absolution

You've sparked the phrases that signified salvation

To have broken what restrained the torrent of feeling and thought which then rushed forth in fury with intensity large

And uncontrollable

Skies in the throes of storm

The scream within the squall

How well contained then was I,

Still all the words kept safe in surplus not enough

As there exists not for me an adequate description for what it is
to live within the safety of your love

Blinding

Turbid and beautiful

All the while lost within my own

The love I construct for you

To have taken the tangled webs I've woven over the course of
years

Strands of shields knitted of thin air

Crafted for safety,

Slices of comfort

Fashioned now into a home

With the hope that your spirit might come to nest within the
warmth of the hope I possess for us

Wear

To rest eyes as weary

Heavy of head and spirit

An undeniable need

Knotted limbs pulled clumsily to an earth grappling at worn heels with the strong hands of gravity

Heaving exasperated sighs

This crippling inability

Memories to mark the shape of who I've now become

A girl made of clay now fired solid by the heat of heartache

Reliving those searing seconds

Cuts in the fabric of time

Astounding accuracy

Drawn back into the lucidity of years passed

Standing as an epitaph belonging to your mind

Now a piece of your living spirit stored within

Seams as scars etched upon outstretched palms in symbol and psalm

Road maps of where you've been

A chronicle of shadows you've stood in

Reflections of splintered mirrors exposing the innocent lost

Label it regret

Damnation

To think you were once entrusted with
everything I was

Then to have built myself around your dreams

In complete faith

And undying loyalty

In duty and service to your whim

To complete the tasks born of your hands

The hands pressed heavy upon this flesh

A willing captive?

Producing for you trinkets of flesh and days passed

Crafting offerings

Symbols and tokens of what I had hoped to draw from life and gift unto you

Shreds of wishes I stacked to fabricate our nest of make believe

Fragile as to dissolve once light fell upon the realization of our fears

Illuminating the harsh realities of a desperate existence with no planned escape

Trying to forge a clear exit

Pathways to bore through clay, tunnels in stone

I living always in the crosshairs of your well-honed hatred

A target deemed worthy of a rage cunning and sadistic enough
to have been bred

By only you

And still I granted to you my allegiance, unwavering in solidity as
you stole the breath of life from my tired body one shallow gasp
at a time,
smiling as you submerged me,
laughing as I struggled,
waiting patiently until the battle's end,
to witness my loss turned your sweet victory

I looked upon you with fond remembrance of what you'd once
done in the name of my
honor while you pressed weak limbs to flame,

Set to lick the skin

To brand and blister

Sear and scar

I'll stand now and always in remembrance of the face of the cru-
elty with which you regarded me, and fail

To understand why

The Assigned

Where, may I ask, have you been?

Through the difficult days and endless nights

The trials

The tears

The heartache and hopelessness?

While you looked the other way, in the vacuum of your absence

All I had was the hope that you were still close enough to hear
the screams of the
innocent

Victims of circumstance and man's ugliest tendencies

Betrayed by your negligence

Sacrificed to the Gods of your irresponsibility

The hope that you might someday come to know a pain unbear-
able such as ours

How you'll feel

With wings set ablaze by small hands, tiny   fingers
Sufferings that make you pray for the salvation you callously
denied the faultless

Only to find their same empty hours

And unanswered prayers

Attain a true understanding of abjection

The great driving force of the faithless, their apathy and torpor,
you as their shepherd

Reformed as Wolf

Adam

I'm watching the smooth movements of your mouth framing phrases in the dark

A welcomed transition from the blissful silence we lay upon

Your voice forming words in whispers, meant to illustrate what you and I share silently as knowledge already

What we embrace as unspoken fact

To give a name to what has come to exist between the fast enclosing stretch between you and I.....

And I

I attempt to draw maps...

Descriptions of my navigations through the exhilaration of this terrain

Vast and incredible

To chronicle an earth of hearts now fully formed

In ink

I accomplish mere stumbles... in fits and starts and little more

To chart a land so new, perhaps just so well preserved, as to have just been graced with the single flag

Waving victoriously

Announcing a claimed territory of the previously unbroken earth beneath

Cradling in embrace the woven declaration waving above

Emblazoned with your name

This land won through battle

The battle of earth's longstanding heart-sickness – to have almost overcome us with sorrows immeasurable

Still we render ourselves victorious in the miraculousness of our shared strength

Though not to be forgotten, the wounds of this previous war

We wear our scars as staunch reminders of the decades past

Yet still finding comfort in recovery

In the shelter of one another

We write the code of a new country

Erecting rules as we move along

Naming them as we see fit

Others simply birthing themselves into titles they were destined to bear

Here is peace

Next, temperance

Now Love

Desire is ours and ours alone
It is its own law

Not written, nor destined

It is the energy promoted between us

Our touch breathing life into it at its very origin

Feeding it as a force

We are how it came to be

This and so much else

Your immaculate words

So applicable here

How right you always are

You are king and I queen of a world invented by our ever growing
need for one another

Gods in a universe of our own creation

Housing continents made up of us as an entity
where earthly sounds go muted to an all-encompassing hush

Miniature streams of fresh water raining down, cold from over-
head

Falling on ears thrust into a state of temporary deafness in the
wake of unspeakable ecstasy

I looking into you with eyes replaced by pools awestruck to the
color of desert twilight

To follow hope

Absolute hope

You and I sampling from energy strengthened into tangibility

Then weaving its strands into invisible castles of thin air that
sketch themselves as magic

Blueprints of unimaginable beauty – each perfect unto itself and
unique in its entirety

We will soon gaze upon the welcoming horizon

To rest our eyes on these monuments

To smile as they build themselves before us

Effigies of strength and solidity

Where we shall rest out souls

Yes,

My beloved –

You are king

And I queen

And everything you see before you is ours

Everything you see before you is us

Exhaustion

Kneading away with hands bloodied and shaking from effort's excess

Fervor to serve as exhaustion's precursor

Security as wanton fallacy

Miserable and wasted

These attempts to make sustenance from stones

As well your hands' ability to safely hold water

Your broken understanding of the ways of this nation

As greed reigns where greatness once lay

And your most pristine loves now just dumping grounds for your angst's toxicity and the ugliness of your indiscretions

But the fight of this weak flesh against current or coast saves not your body from the pull of the violent tide

And to lay waste to that which you hold dear

Brings about only the necessity of suffering alone

To feel now the sting of sweat upon eyes

Bring tear onto wound

And receive no absolution in your quest for comfort or shelter

Your only recourse a prayer for strength

To face the hardship or an end to the need for such resiliencies

Something in the way of a celestial pardon

Time to rest

Peace of mind

Love

The ability to accomplish

A physical dexterity

Proud as to carry my own weight

The proverbial soft place to land

Assistance without indignity

The beauty of partnership and a resurrection of faith

Light

To the grace and eloquence that radiated from that blissful light
living within you

Shining resplendence

Beauty cradled in soft downy hope

A splendor called your soul

You rose and brought with you the bliss of completion

A warmth that carried me

And how you were the sun in my earth

You've been the keeper of joys both great and small

Bearing the blessing of unbridled happiness to bestow upon the
rest of the world

All standing eagerly in attention

In hopes as to be whispered to by the touch of the light of your
sweet presence

19

Farewell

Living as the cover of a morning

Thick white to swallow a day in springtime

Where breeze stirs circles into foliage

Wishes gone stale now adrift upon fresh clusters of cherry blossom

Cotton candy pink

Honeysuckle sweet

The draw of you to me

The skin you wore,

An extension of mine

My blood yours as well;

Hope and dreams afloat within

No comfort here without pain

No gain or glory
Without loss

We were the swords

The suit we were born to brandish

How we cut both ways

Celebrations not without tragedy

And how right you were –

This pain is just too real

A memory to fit in this keepsake box

The last you wept in my arms

And promises you made of what heaven would look like once your
spirit laid claim to it

The sound of your laughter yet to be extinguished

Still ringing in my ears

Completion

Where your loyalties lay

Burns the mind

Stains a heart

What love might sing beauty

May also scream fire

To slay these days and light your nights

Run screaming your soul

A hammer to the innocent

Record the pound of a pulse

Haunting Rhetoric

What you create with your blood

A buffer to the passage of time built in your image

Growing a garden of unexpected challenge
Procuring a battle of new wills

Long enough to file down your resistances

Hang weights upon your spirit

Cry you the call of the kindred,

Loose the wolves in the sugar cane

Sleep sweet, vast fields of clover, nestled in the keep of a warm
summer earth

Hone your meager defenses to the impending army of winged
terror

And recall the scorched year of your birth

I'll summon you into my physical fold like the billowy sweet smell
of sun baked linen in an early spring to the senses of a child rapt
with the thrill of discovery's delights

Our deficiencies will live as one, double negatives then to posi-
tives

As dictates the physical world

And we are left as one to stand, to mature with time's whispers
of evolution, rebirth, and decay

Finding our splendid unification

Caressed with the wane of personal winters, realized as the
eve of the lush and succulent,

To bloom into rare and coveted security, the affect of genuine
love

And wither us then to one and one another in our autumn's em-
ber's slow fade

Blessed with the magic of reminiscence

And the completion of an illustrious work.

Author Bio:

Jessica Mannes is a wife and mother with strong beliefs and a lust for life itself. She has learned important lessons in bleak circumstances, most importantly thankfulness for every opportunity and how to wear battle scars with grace and dignity. She currently resides in Buffalo, New York and is employed in the field of human services.